T0061069

WORLD WINDOWS

Animals Move

HEINLE CENGAGE Learning™

Y|S|G A YBM COMPANY Young & Son Global, Inc.

How does your pet move?

Contents

Vocabulary	4
Move	6
Hop	7
Run	8
Jump	10
Swing	11
Swim	12
Fly	13
Summary	14
Song	15
Index	16

Vocabulary
hop
run
jump

swing
swim
fly

Animals move in different ways. Animals use their body parts to move.

A kangaroo has legs.
A kangaroo hops with its legs.

A cheetah has legs, too.
A cheetah runs with its legs.

A frog has legs, too.
A frog jumps with its legs.

An orangutan has arms.
An orangutan swings with its arms.

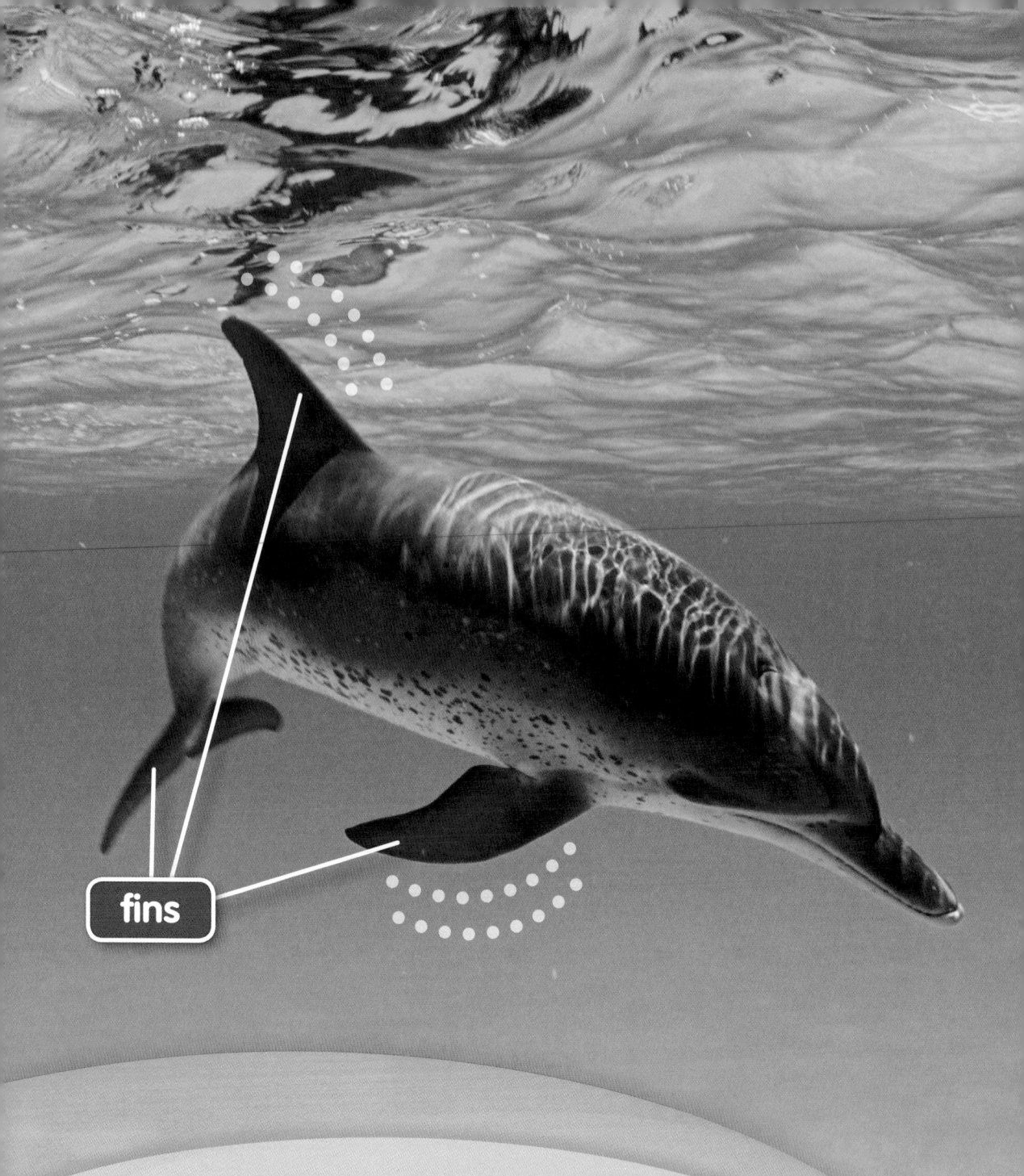

A dolphin has fins.
A dolphin swims with its fins.

An eagle has wings.
An eagle flies with its wings.
wings

Summary

How do these animals move?

Song

How Do Animals Move?

Look at the animals. How do they move?
Cheetahs run, and kangaroos hop.
Frogs jump, and orangutans swing.
How about eagles and dolphins?

Look at the animals. How do they move?
Cheetahs run, and kangaroos hop.
Frogs jump, and orangutans swing.
How about eagles and dolphins?

Index

animals, 6

arms, 11

fins, 12

flies, 13

hops, 7

jumps, 10

legs, 6–8, 10

move, 6

runs, 8

swims, 12

swings, 11

wings, 13